D0570947

RACE FOR HISTORY

WHO REACHED THE SOUTH POLE FIRST?

by Sheila Griffin Llanas

Consultant:
John Splettstoesser
Polar Consultant
International Association of
Antarctica Tour Operators

CAPSTONE PRESS
a capstone imprint

Fact Finders are published by Capstone Press,
151 Good Counsel Drive, P.O. Box 669, Mankato, Minnesota 56002.
www.capstonepub.com

Books published by Capstone Press are manufactured with paper
containing at least 10 percent post-consumer waste.

Library of Congress Cataloging-in-Publication Data
Llanas, Sheila Griffin, 1958–
  Who reached the South Pole first? / by Sheila Griffin Llanas.
  p. cm.—(Fact finders. Race for history)
  Includes bibliographical references and index.
  Summary: "Follows the stories of Roald Amundsen and Robert Falcon Scott, as they
race across Antarctica toward the South Pole"—Provided by publisher.
  ISBN 978-1-4296-3344-4 (library binding)
  ISBN 978-1-4296-6245-1 (paperback)
  1. Amundsen, Roald, 1872-1928—Travel—Juvenile literature. 2. Scott, Robert Falcon, 1868-1912—
Travel—Juvenile literature. 3. Antarctica—Discovery and exploration—Juvenile literature. 4. South
Pole—Discovery and exploration—Juvenile literature. I. Title. II. Series.
  G850 1912 .A48 L55 2011
  919.8'9—dc22
                                                                      2010026027

Editorial Credits
Jennifer Besel, editor; Alison Thiele, series designer; Bobbie Nuytten, book designer;
    Wanda Winch, media researcher; Eric Manske, production specialist

Photo Credits
Alamy Images: Classic Image, cover (top), 16, Interfoto/Personalities, 5 (bottom), North Wind Picture
Archives, 22, Photos12, 18, Pictorial Press Ltd, 12, Royal Geographical Society/H.R. Bowers, 25; Corbis,
5 (top), Bettmann, 15; Getty Images: Popperfoto, cover (bottom), 19, 21; Library of Congress: Prints
and Photographs Division, 8, 20; Mary Evans Picture Library: Illustrated London News Ltd, 6; Nova
Development Corporation, 28-29 (icons); Shutterstock: ducu59us, 28 (London), U.P. images, (banner);
NOAA: Steve Nicklas, 10; Wikipedia: Herbert George Ponting, 9

Printed in the United States of America in Stevens Point, Wisconsin.
092010   005934WZS11

TABLE OF CONTENTS

THE RACE

Antarctica remains a place of vast wilderness and untold adventure. For years, explorers have skirted its icy borders. Seal hunters brave its seas' high winds and choppy waters. Explorers steer close to its coast to chart huge cliffs of ice.

But one spot on this frozen land is still untouched by humankind—the South Pole. Fierce cold has kept explorers from reaching the very bottom of planet Earth. Now in 1909, explorers are pulled like magnets to the center of Antarctica. They will race through wicked cold and risk death to be first to the pole. Only one team will win. Who will it be?

ROALD AMUNDSEN

A 38-year-old explorer from Norway—he has trained on skis in the Norwegian mountains. He's studied the ways of the Inuit, the Arctic's native people. Amundsen has traveled to both the Arctic and Antarctica.

ROBERT FALCON SCOTT

A 42-year-old naval officer from England—he tried and failed to reach the South Pole in 1901. This failure only fuels his desire to achieve the goal.

CHAPTER ONE
PREPARING FOR THE POLE

Failure Pushes Him On

Robert Scott is not a man who gives up easily. A loyal and dedicated young man, Scott rose quickly in the ranks of the British Navy. By the age of 18, he was promoted to officer. Scott's hardworking nature and leadership skills caught the eye of geographer Sir Clements Markham. Markham chose Scott to lead his Antarctic exploration. Scott had never thought of going to Antarctica before. But it was an opportunity too good to pass up.

In 1901 Scott hired a crew to help him reach the South Pole. He chose British Lieutenant Ernest Shackleton and Dr. Edward Wilson to go with him. The men pushed their way through the icy land. They brushed death time and again. Still they pushed on. But progress was slow—too slow. A low supply of food and **scurvy** quickly made progress impossible. More than 480 **nautical miles** (889 kilometers) from the pole, the men turned back. The South Pole remained untouched. But Scott wasn't about to give up.

Shackleton, Scott, and Wilson

scurvy: an illness caused by poor diet

nautical mile: the unit used to measure distance by Antarctic explorers

the *Terra Nova*

Now it is 1909. Last year, Shackleton got 97 miles (180 km) from the pole. Scott decides to try again. With the little money he has, Scott buys an old ship called the *Terra Nova*. It's not the boat he wants, but it will have to do. Then he gathers a crew. More than 8,000 men volunteer. Scott chooses 65 men, including sailors, geologists, and a photographer.

One of Scott's biggest decisions is about transportation on the ice. On his first Antarctic trip, he used sled dogs. But the dogs all got sick. Scott thinks ponies will do better. He also decides to bring **motor sledges** to use on the ice.

motor sledge: a vehicle that runs on a spiked track and is steered by ropes

On June 1, 1910, the *Terra Nova* is loaded with food, equipment, and three motor sledges. The crew leaves London with a hope for adventure and a prayer to return home.

Four months later, the *Terra Nova* arrives in Melbourne, Australia. Scott receives a telegram. It's from Roald Amundsen, an explorer from Norway. The message says Amundsen is on his way to the South Pole. Scott's trip has just become a race!

The *Terra Nova* has one more stop to make. In Lyttelton, New Zealand, they pick up 19 ponies and 33 dogs. With so many people and animals onboard, the ship is overcrowded. Scott feels a sense of doom. Why didn't anyone know what Amundsen was planning?

the crew of the *Terra Nova*

A Quick Change in Plans

Roald Amundsen is a hardened explorer. He survived an Antarctic winter when his ship was frozen into the ice. He is an expert skier, and he's studied the Inuit's way of life.

Now in 1909, Amundsen's goal is to be first to reach the North Pole. As Amundsen gets ready, he learns that Englishman Robert Scott is planning a trip to the South Pole.

the *Fram*

The king of Norway gives Amundsen money for his journey. Amundsen's friend Fridtjof Nansen, a fellow explorer, lends him a ship called the *Fram*. Amundsen hires a crew of 19 skilled explorers and sailors, including an ice pilot. The ice pilot will steer the ship around icebergs and through **pack ice**.

But just as plans are coming together, the news breaks. Someone else has claimed the North Pole! With the North Pole taken, Amundsen makes a quick decision. He plans to sail to the South Pole. But he tells no one of his new plans. On August 9, 1910, the *Fram* leaves Norway, stocked with supplies and dogs. Everyone thinks the explorers are headed to the North Pole to do research.

One month later, the ship docks at Madeira Island off the western coast of Africa. Amundsen calls his crew to deck. As the men line up, Amundsen reveals his secret. The *Fram* is sailing south. The shocked crewmen stand in silence. Amundsen gives each man a last chance to quit. His mind races, wondering if they will stay onboard or if his trick will backfire.

RACE FACT

Two people actually claimed the North Pole. Robert Peary and Frederick Cook both claimed the win.

pack ice: chunks of frozen seawater drifting on the surface of the ocean

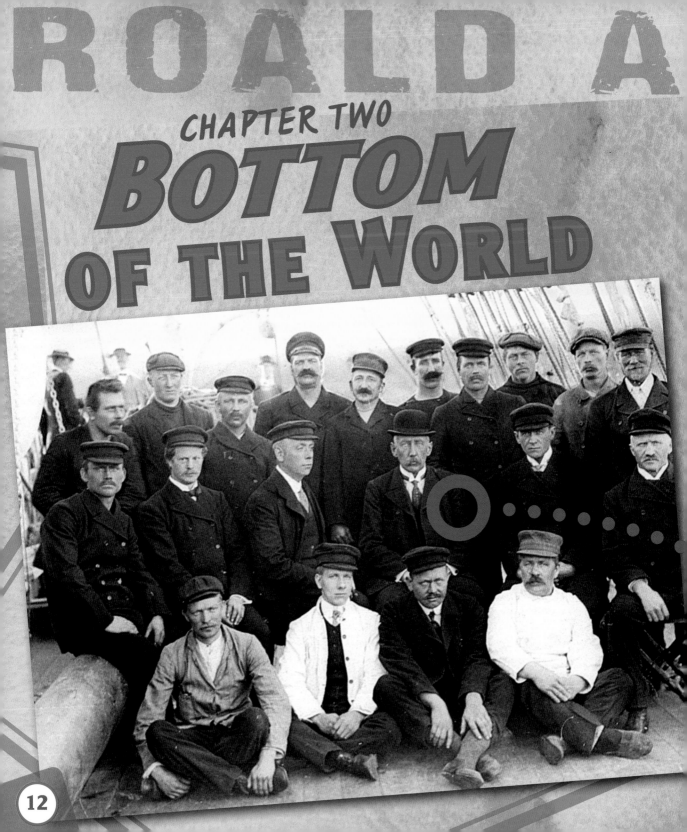

Amundsen Gets His Answer

Amundsen holds his breath as he waits for his crewmen's answers. He needs every one of them.

The loyal crew does not leave Amundsen. Every man stays. As the *Fram* sets sail, Amundsen's brother posts a telegram to Australia. The message is meant for Captain Robert Scott. It says Amundsen is going to the South Pole.

Onboard the *Fram*, the crewmen prepare themselves for a different journey. They rebuild their sleds so they will glide smoothly on the ice. They stitch tents to keep out the cold. They even build a blacksmith shop and make harnesses for the 97 howling sled dogs.

Amundsen insists the dogs be treated well. He rations the men's freshwater so the dogs can have all they want. The men go without butter so the dogs can eat it to gain weight. Amundsen is convinced that without healthy dogs, his mission will not succeed.

Amundsen (middle with round hat) and his crew on the *Fram*

RACE FACT

Each crewman was in charge of caring for and training six or seven dogs. When 21 puppies were born at sea, the men had to care for even more dogs.

AMUNDSEN

The *Fram* arrives in Antarctica on January 14, 1911. Amundsen chooses a spot in the Bay of Whales for base camp. No one has ever started the journey to the pole from here.

Quickly the men get to work. They must get much done before winter. Crewmen unload the ship. They hunt seals and bury the meat in snow to preserve it. They also build a hut to protect themselves through the long winter. Once camp is ready, the men make short trips into Antarctica, bringing food and fuel with them. They stock three **depots** full of supplies for Amundsen to use on his trip to the South Pole.

Eight men stay with Amundsen at base camp through the long, dark winter. The men stay busy caring for the dogs. As the end of winter nears, the men are anxious to get moving. But storms and dangerously low temperatures keep them shut inside. Amundsen worries about his chances of making it to the pole first. He could lose if Scott's team has already left.

depot: a shelter and supply station for the team to use on the way to and from the pole

a motor sledge

Scott Lands on the Ice

Scott and his men land in Antarctica on January 4, 1911, only four months before the bitter Antarctic winter. Right away, things don't go as they hoped. As they unload the supplies, a motor sledge breaks through the ice and sinks. One month after arriving in Antarctica, a team leaves to survey the coast. The *Terra Nova* sails past the *Fram*. Amundsen is here!

On April 21, the sun sets. The dark Antarctic winter has arrived. The men spend the winter on Antarctica, preparing for their trip to the pole. Scott worries about the journey. And he wonders what Amundsen is planning.

CHAPTER THREE
RACE TO THE POLE

Amundsen and his sled dogs

Amundsen Off and Running

It's October 19, and the weather is finally right for Amundsen's team to set out. He brings his four best men, Olav Bjaaland, Helmer Hanssen, Sverre Hassel, and Oscar Wisting. Four sleds loaded with four months of supplies are pulled by 52 healthy sled dogs.

The team pushes through blowing snow and fog. The men can barely see the dogs in front of them. They can't see the **crevasses** in the ice. They narrowly avoid death several times.

Then the men push their way over the mountains that block the path to the pole. They make it over the mountains safely. They have been traveling for more than a month. Amundsen and his men must do a chore they have been dreading. They need more food for the dogs that will go to the pole. The men shoot 24 dogs. The meat from those dogs will be fed to the others. The men are sad to lose the dogs. But they know they have no choice if they want to succeed.

RACE FACT
Each of Amundsen's sleds weighed 880 pounds (399 kg). They were loaded with pemmican, dried milk, chocolate, biscuits, tents, and fuel.

crevasse: a deep crack in a glacier

Days later, their sorrow turns to joy. They glide past the spot Shackleton reached on his expedition in 1908. Only 97 nautical miles (180 km) to go! Amundsen's eyes fill with tears. He is close, so close. As the team continues on, they look for any sign of Scott. Is it possible that Scott is ahead of them?

Amundsen and his team crossing the Axel Heiberg Glacier

Scott's team packing sleds for the trip

Scott's Second Try

On November 1, Scott begins his second journey across Antarctica. He sets out with 16 men, two motor sledges, 10 ponies, 23 dogs, and 13 sleds packed with supplies. Scott tells the men that only three will go with him all the way to the pole. But no one knows who will be chosen. Those who aren't chosen will help stock depots with food and fuel for the return trip. Then they and the dogs will go back to base camp.

Wilson, Scott, Evans,
Oates, and Bowers

The trip does not go smoothly from the start. After a week, the motor sledges break down and are left on the ice. Howling blizzards bury the tents in snow, stopping the men for days at a time. When they reach the Beardmore Glacier, the men are forced to shoot the weak ponies. They save the meat to eat later. When the team gets 170 miles (315 km) from the pole, Scott chooses his final team. Instead of three men, he chooses four. Edward Wilson, Lawrence Oates, Edgar Evans, and Henry Bowers will be Scott's team to the pole. But Scott only packed enough supplies for four men.

Scott's team crossing the Beardmore Glacier

Without horses or dogs, the men put on the harnesses and pull the sleds themselves. The work is difficult and slow. They struggle over ice and plunge through knee-deep snow. As the days go by, they suffer from weakness, **snow blindness**, and hunger.

The men cross the silent land, thinking of their goal. They wonder about Amundsen. Where is he? And is he having this much trouble?

snow blindness: a painful condition of the eyes caused by the light reflected on the snow

CHAPTER FOUR
THE END OF A JOURNEY

Amundsen (left)
checking his position
at the South Pole

Amundsen Yells Halt!

Amundsen hasn't seen any sign of Scott's team. Hope that he's in the lead fills his heart. It's December 14, 1911. It's been two months since they left base camp. The men watch their sledge meters, knowing they are close to their goal. Suddenly, the men shout "Halt!" at the same time. Every sledge meter has marked the spot. This is the South Pole! The men raise the Norwegian flag. It's clear that no one else has been here. Have they won the race?

The team camps at the South Pole for three days. Amundsen writes two letters to leave at the pole. One letter is for Norway's king, claiming the win for Norway. The other letter is for Robert Scott, wishing him luck on his return journey. Then the men pack up and head back across the icy land. They have fine weather, and their high spirits push them on. All five men return healthy and strong to base camp. They board the *Fram* and leave to tell the world of their accomplishment.

RACE FACT

Amundsen and his team traveled about 1,400 nautical miles (2,593 km) to the South Pole and back.

Scott Sees a Flag

Scott and his teammates grow weak from hunger and hauling the sleds. Each day is a struggle to survive. They left base camp more than two months ago. They know they're close to the pole. Then on January 17, 1912, the men spot a flag waving against the background of the white world. As Scott draws closer, he sees the remains of a camp. Amundsen was here. The men are deeply disappointed. They have reached the pole, only to be beaten in the race.

The only thing left to do is return to base camp. Cold, hungry, and exhausted, the men wonder if they can make it back.

Luck is not on their side. For almost two months, the men fight their way through wicked storms. They shiver in temperatures dropping to minus 47 degrees Fahrenheit (minus 44 degrees Celsius). Scott falls and hurts his shoulder. A snow-blind Wilson hurts his leg. Oates can barely put his boots on over his **frostbitten** toes. The food is running out. The men are near starvation.

frostbite: damage to the body caused by extreme cold

RACE FACT

Scott and his men were so cold and weak that it took them 90 minutes just to put on their boots.

Scott (far left) and his team by the tent Amundsen left at the pole

The tired men weave their way around deep crevasses in the ice. Evans falls and hits his head. He dies as the men pull him on a sled. A few days later, Oates is too weak to go on. He wakes from sleep and leaves the tent. He never comes back. Then on March 29, a blizzard traps Scott, Wilson, and Bowers in their tent. They have no fuel and only a bit of food. Their strength and their hope is gone. All five men in Scott's team die in Antarctica.

THE WINNER

Both Amundsen and Scott wanted to be the first to the South Pole. But only one could win. Amundsen reached the pole on December 14, 1911, becoming the winner of the race. Scott arrived at the pole 34 days later, on January 17, 1912. Only Amundsen's team survived to tell of their amazing journey. Scott's story is known through the many journal entries he made on his long, hard trip. Today both Roald Amundsen and Robert Falcon Scott are honored for their amazing courage on their race to the South Pole.

RACE FACT

Scott, Wilson, and Bowers died 11 miles (20 km) from a depot stocked with food and fuel. They just didn't have the strength to get there.

LEGEND

━━ AMUNDSEN'S PATH
━━ SCOTT'S PATH
● BASE CAMPS
⛰ GLACIERS
∧ TRANSANTARCTIC MOUNTAINS
✛ SOUTH POLE

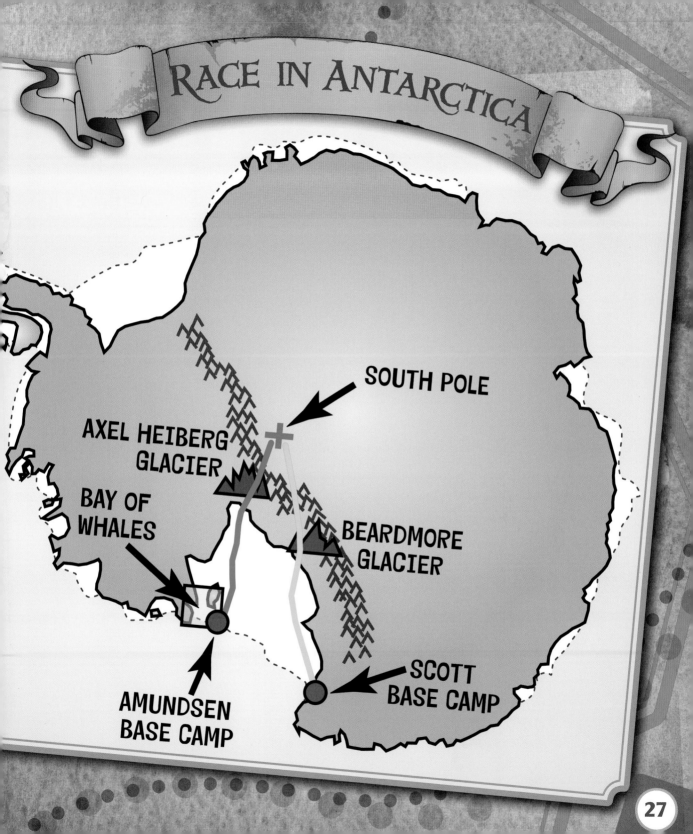

RACE IN ANTARCTICA

SOUTH POLE

AXEL HEIBERG
GLACIER

BAY OF
WHALES

BEARDMORE
GLACIER

SCOTT
BASE CAMP

AMUNDSEN
BASE CAMP

TIMELINE

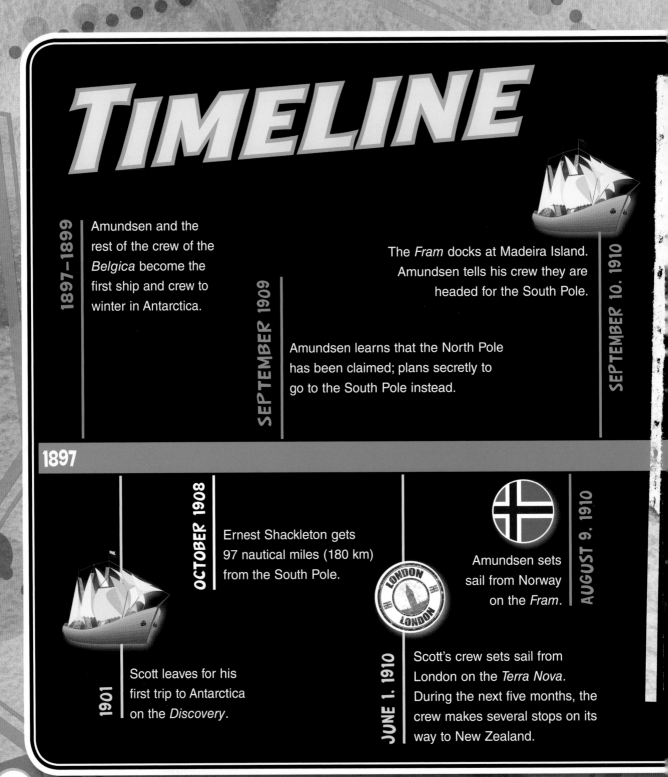

1897–1899
Amundsen and the rest of the crew of the *Belgica* become the first ship and crew to winter in Antarctica.

SEPTEMBER 1909
Amundsen learns that the North Pole has been claimed; plans secretly to go to the South Pole instead.

SEPTEMBER 10. 1910
The *Fram* docks at Madeira Island. Amundsen tells his crew they are headed for the South Pole.

1897

OCTOBER 1908
Ernest Shackleton gets 97 nautical miles (180 km) from the South Pole.

1901
Scott leaves for his first trip to Antarctica on the *Discovery*.

AUGUST 9. 1910
Amundsen sets sail from Norway on the *Fram*.

JUNE 1. 1910
Scott's crew sets sail from London on the *Terra Nova*. During the next five months, the crew makes several stops on its way to New Zealand.

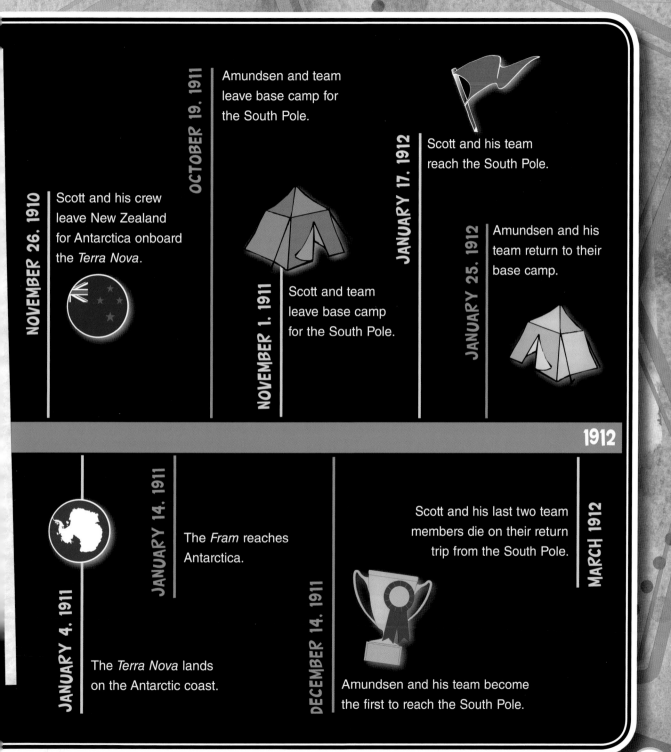

OCTOBER 19, 1911
Amundsen and team leave base camp for the South Pole.

NOVEMBER 26, 1910
Scott and his crew leave New Zealand for Antarctica onboard the *Terra Nova*.

NOVEMBER 1, 1911
Scott and team leave base camp for the South Pole.

JANUARY 17, 1912
Scott and his team reach the South Pole.

JANUARY 25, 1912
Amundsen and his team return to their base camp.

1912

JANUARY 14, 1911
The *Fram* reaches Antarctica.

JANUARY 4, 1911
The *Terra Nova* lands on the Antarctic coast.

DECEMBER 14, 1911
Amundsen and his team become the first to reach the South Pole.

MARCH 1912
Scott and his last two team members die on their return trip from the South Pole.

GLOSSARY

crevasse (kruh-VAS)—a deep crack in the surface of a glacier

depot (DEE-poh)—a shelter and supply station that teams set up to use on the way to and from the pole

frostbite (FRAWST-byt)—a condition that occurs when cold temperatures freeze skin

motor sledge (MO-tuhr SLEG)—a tanklike vehicle that ran on a spiked track and was steered by ropes; the experimental vehicle could go a top speed of 3.5 miles (5.6 km) per hour

nautical mile (NAW-tuh-kuhl MILE)—a unit for measuring distance; one nautical mile equals 6,076 feet (1.9 km)

pack ice (PAK EYESS)—chunks of frozen seawater drifting on the surface of the ocean

pemmican (PEH-mi-kuhn)—lean meat that is pounded until fine and then mixed with melted fat

scurvy (SKUR-vee)—a deadly disease caused by a lack of vitamin C; scurvy causes swollen limbs, bleeding gums, and great weakness

snow blindness (SNO BLIND-nuhs)—swelling in the eyes caused by exposure to ultraviolet rays reflected off snow and ice

telegram (TEL-uh-gram)—a message sent by telegraph; a telegraph sends electrical signals by wire or radio over long distances

READ MORE

Friedman, Mel. *Antarctica.* A True Book. New York: Children's Press, 2009.

Gogerly, Liz. *Amundsen and Scott's Race to the South Pole.* Great Journeys across Earth. Chicago: Heinemann Library, 2008.

Thompson, Gare. *Roald Amundsen and Robert Scott Race to the South Pole.* National Geographic History Chapters. Washington, D.C.: National Geographic, 2007.

INTERNET SITES

FactHound offers a safe, fun way to find Internet sites related to this book. All of the sites on FactHound have been researched by our staff.

Here's all you do:

Visit *www.facthound.com*

Type in this code: 9781429633444

Super-cool stuff!

Check out projects, games and lots more at
www.capstonekids.com

INDEX